INTERNATIONAL TERRORISM

Richard Edwards

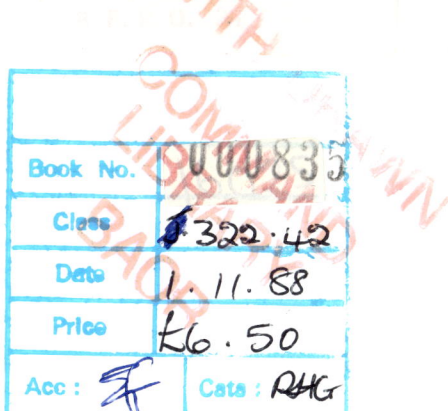

World Issues

Frontispiece: A masked Shiite Muslim hijacker negotiates the release of 39 hostages aboard the TWA jet at Beirut, Lebanon 1985.
Cover: Palestinian guerillas, armed and wearing combat gear, see themselves as freedom fighters and not as terrorists.

Editor: Tim Byrne
Designer: Ross George

First published in 1988 by
Wayland (Publishers) Ltd
61 Western Road, Hove
East Sussex, BN3 1JD, England

British Library Cataloguing in Publication Data
Edwards, Richard
   International Terrorism – (World Issues)
   1. International Terrorism
   I. Title   II. Series
   322.4'2
   ISBN 1–85210–144–X

Phototypeset by Kalligraphics Ltd., Redhill, Surrey
Printed and bound in Italy by Sagdos S.p.A., Milan

Contents

1
Years of Violence

In today's world, no one is innocent and no one is neutral.
George Habash, leader of the PFLP

It will not be a clean or pleasant fight.
George Schultz, US Secretary of State

Open the pages of a newspaper, or watch a news programme on the television, and you will almost certainly find a report of events in which terrorism plays a central role. Almost every day it is possible to find news of an incident related to terrorism. It may be a gun attack in India, a bomb exploding in Spain, or the kidnapping of hostages in Lebanon. Terrorism is now part of our daily lives.

During the last twenty years, new terrorist groups have sprung up around the world. Governments have had little success in their attempts to resolve disputes in which terrorism is used. The situation in northern Spain is a good example. The Euzkadi ta Azkatazuna (ETA) began its struggle for a separate Basque state while Spain was ruled by the fascist dictator General Franco. When Spain returned to democracy after his death, many of the demands of ETA were met. However, they still continue their campaign for a completely separate Basque homeland. In fact, they have been more active militarily since the return to democracy than they were while Franco was alive.

The spread of terrorism

ETA, the Palestine Liberation Organization (PLO) and the Provisional Irish Republican Army (IRA) are well-established groups who have engaged in acts of terrorism over a number of years. New groups, particularly in

The Spanish separatist movement ETA, formed in 1959, has organized many strikes and protests to further its campaign for a separate state.

The PLO hijacked three planes at Dawson's Airfield, Jordan in 1970. By blowing up all of the planes the PLO gained wider publicity.

developing countries, have emerged more recently. Nations which have become independent of colonial rule since the Second World War are now experiencing the growth of separatist movements within their own borders. Some Sikhs in India and Tamils in Sri Lanka have taken up arms against their governments in attempts to form their own states.

We have witnessed aeroplanes being hijacked and blown up. Leading politicians, diplomats and business people have been kidnapped. Some have been returned after the payment of a ransom, or after the release of terrorist prisoners. Some have been killed. In 1978 the Italian Red Brigade kidnapped the former Prime Minister Aldo Moro. Several weeks later, having been tried in a 'People's court', he was found, shot dead in the boot of a car. Some attacks have been unsuccessful,

In 1978 the Italian Red Brigade kidnapped the former Prime Minister, Aldo Moro. Their unmet demands led to Moro being killed.

7

KEY TO ORGANIZATIONS

1 FMLN (Farabundio Marti National Liberation Front)

2 Contras

3 M 19

4 Sendero Luminoso

5 MR-8

6 IRA (Irish Republican Army)

7 INLA (Irish National Liberation Army)

8 UVF (Ulster Volunteer Force)

9 CCC (Fighting Communist Cells)

10 Red Army Fraction

11 Action Directe

12 ETA (Euzkadi Ta Azkatazuna)

13 FP 25

14 Red Brigades

15 Abu Nidal Group

16 Asala (Armenian Secret Army)

17 Islamic Jihad — Hizb Allah

18 PLO (Palestine Liberation Organization)

19 PFLP (Popular Front for the Liberation of Palestine)

20 Mujaheddin

21 Sikh groups

22 LTTE (Liberation Tigers of Tamil Eeelam)

23 SWAPO (South West Africa People's Organization)

24 MNR (Renamo)

25 ANC (African National Congress)

26 ELF (Eritrean Liberation Front)

1985 M19 seizure of the Supreme Court in Colombia

1979 Iranian embassy, London
stormed by SAS

1984
Brighton bombing by IRA

UNITED
KINGDOM
1969
Bloody Sunday
7   8
IRELAND
6
9
BELG **W**
FRANCE **GERMANY**
11 **10**
ROM
1980 Bologna railway bombing by
Red Army
12
SPAIN
14
13
PORTUGAL
TURKEY **16**
1970 Explosion of 3 hi-jacked
planes at Dawson's field
Jordan
18
19 **17**
IRAN
20
1984 Prime Minister Indira Gandhi
killed by militant Sikhs
LIBYA
1985
Failed attempt to retake
Egypt Air 737 at Malta
15
21
1986
Raid on Libya by U.S. Air
Force
INDIA
26
ETHIOPIA
SOMALIA
22
SRI LANKA
UGANDA
1976
Raid on Entebbe
1977 Raid on Mogadishu
MALAWI
24
23
MOZAMBIQUE
NAMIBIA
25
1960 Sharpeville protests
1976 Soweto uprising
SOUTH AFRICA

AUSTRALIA

NEW ZEALAND

9

such as the placing of a bomb by the PIRA in the Brighton hotel where the British Conservative Cabinet was staying in 1984. Others, such as the assassination of Prime Minister Indira Gandhi of India, have succeeded.

Terrorism is perceived to be on the increase, making the world less safe than it was twenty years ago. We are encouraged to be more watchful when we travel, particularly when flying abroad; we cannot be absolutely sure that a bomb will not go off when we are shopping; our political leaders have increased security to protect themselves. So it often seems that no-one is safe from the bomb or bullet. But should we worry about terrorism as much as we do?

Terrorist acts get a lot of news coverage, which possibly increases the scale and significance of their effects. At the same time, the media have not always provided much coverage of important third world issues. In the last twenty years, for example, millions have died from starvation, whereas the number killed in terrorist attacks over the same period is only in the thousands.

In 1984 the IRA attempted to blow up the British Prime Minister and Cabinet who were staying at the Grand Hotel in Brighton, England.

The aftermath of a bomb attack by Tamils in Sri Lanka. Tamil separatists want to form a separate state from the rest of Sri Lanka in the northern province of Jaffna.

International terrorism

The importance given to terrorism has increased as more attacks have taken place in Western Europe. During the 1970s, links were forged between revolutionary groups in Europe and nationalist groups in the Middle East. This led to an increase in the range of terrorist attacks. It was particularly significant that, at this time, the PLO moved its struggle against Israel to Israeli targets in Europe. Links were developed with groups such as the Japanese Red Army and the Baader-Meinhof group in West Germany. International terrorism had entered the ring. Members of the Baader-Meinhof group acted in support of the Palestinian cause. Palestinians took hostages in order to secure the release of their imprisoned European comrades. Joint operations were planned and put into effect. People from all over the world travelled to Palestinian training camps to learn new skills – how to use explosives and arms, or how to falsify documents, for example.

In the mid 1970s, these developments and the concern they generated were summed up in one figure, Carlos. The identity of Carlos was not known until mid-1975. In June of that year, the out very few. The identity of Carlos was not known until mid-1975. In June of that year, the Parisian police visited the flat of Illich Ramirez Sanchez, a Columbian playboy. Sanchez shot dead two of the policemen, wounded a third and shot dead the Palestinian who accompanied them. Investigations revealed that Sanchez was Carlos, the man who had been organizing terrorist attacks throughout Western Europe for the previous two years. The Palestinian who had accompanied the police was Michel Moukharbel. Moukharbel had been the go-between for Carlos and the Popular Front for the Liberation of Palestine (PFLP), a radical Palestinian group.

Operating from Paris, Carlos had worked with the PFLP, the Japanese Red Army, the

In 1972 Kozo Okamoto of the Japanese Red Army was freed in exchange for Israeli prisoners.

The bombing of the railway station in Bologna, Italy in 1980 was the act of the left-wing Red Brigades.

Baader-Meinhof group and the Red Brigades. Yet for all his notoriety, he was involved in organizing only a handful of terrorist attacks. The most notable of these was in 1975 after his real identify had been revealed. In December 1975, a meeting of oil ministers was being held at the Organization of Petroleum Exporting Countries' (OPEC) headquarters in Vienna. It was seized by Carlos and a group including members of the PFLP and Baader-Meinhof. Three security men were shot dead and eleven ministers were taken hostage. The original plan had been to kill the pro-Western ministers from Saudi Arabia and Iran, but in the end a ransom was paid. The kidnappers and hostages were flown to Algeria, where the ministers were released. The kidnappers disappeared. Since then, there have been only two minor incidents in which Carlos is thought to have been involved.

The international connections which the Carlos network illustrated increased concern about terrorism. People could no longer feel safe once they were away from the area of immediate conflict. Attacks could take place anywhere and be carried out by anyone.

The practical links developed between the different groups also led to the exchange of ideas. Groups which were essentially nationalist in their outlook, seeking to gain control of a certain territory, began to take up revolutionary ideas and the pursuit of radical social change. The oppression of the developing world was seen to be maintained by the Western capitalist system. If the nationalist aims of groups such as the PFLP were to be achieved, the capitalist system had to be overthrown.

International terrorism had come of age. Radical groups around the world forged links with one another and with governments who supported their aims, such as Cuba, North Korea and Libya. Terrorism in the 1970s was perceived to be increasingly well-organized, a new and dangerous phenomenon. However, while the degree of co-operation across national boundaries was new, terrorism itself had had a long history.

2
Terrorism in History

In antiquity, the continous struggle for power led to many assassinations. The first recorded terrorist group was the Sicarii in Palestine. The Sicarii was a small religious sect, which fought against Roman rule between AD 66-73. Most of their victims were moderate Jews who were prepared to negotiate with the Romans.

Religion was also important for the Muslim *hashshasin* (from whom we derive the word assassin). Based in Persia, the *hashshasin* fought from the 11th to 13th centuries to maintain their religious freedom. They were a minority sect, and could not win an open war against the majority, so they turned to acts of terrorism to promote their aims. For instance, they killed leading figures in the government, using a particular type of short dagger.

Anarchist movements

While many groups have engaged in terrorism throughout history, the Anarchist political groups in the 19th century are most often remembered. These groups were particularly strong in France, Italy, Spain and the USA, but their roots lay in the Russian People's Will movement.

Anarchists believe that people are basically good natured, and that in the right circumstances everybody can live together in peace and harmony. They oppose the centralized state as an oppressive force which prevents people from co-operating with one another.

The use of terror is not new. In Medieval times, the Spanish Inquisition used torture to extract confessions of guilt from people.

They argue that once the controlling power of the state has been removed, a better, more co-operative society will emerge. The problem facing the Anarchists was how to achieve that better society.

In the 19th century, political activity mostly involved holding political meetings and distributing pamphlets under the constant harassment of agents of the state. The Anarchists turned to violence as a more effective way of promoting social change. This tactic became known as 'propaganda by the deed'. They believed that if the leading figure in the state was killed, the people would see that opposition was possible, and they would rise up in support of the Anarchists and overthrow the whole system. In practice, the Anarchists' use of terror was not very effective. In 1881, a member of the People's Will movement managed to kill Tsar Alexander II, but the people did not rise up to support this action. The movement was heavily suppressed by the next Tsar, and many of its members sought exile in Western Europe where they spread their ideas.

The popular association of terrorism with anarchism is slightly misleading. Many nationalist groups in the 19th century also engaged in acts of terrorism. The Irish Fenians, for example, exploded bombs in London in support of self-rule for Ireland. Armenians and

In 1881, the People's Will movement made an unsuccessful attempt to assassinate Tsar Alexander II of Russia.

Macedonians fought against the Ottoman empire. Similar conflicts continued into the 20th century. In 1914, the heir to the Austrian throne was assassinated in Sarajevo, sparking off the First World War.

In Russia, prior to the 1917 Revolution, terrorism was used by the Social Revolutionaries. This promoted a lot of discussion within the revolutionary movement at the time. Nowadays, terrorism is largely associated in the public mind with left-wing and Marxist-inspired groups, although the major socialist and Marxist leaders have all condemned terrorism as counter-productive. Lenin, the leader of the Bolshevik Party, argued that acts of terrorism provoked greater repression from the Russian state, while at the same time creating hostility towards the revolutionaries among the people who might otherwise support them. This was not a blanket rejection of terrorism, however. Lenin also argued that acts of terrorism could be used as a tool of the revolutionary movement, but only as a small part of its overall activities.

Terrorism has often been justified by its perpetrators because they believe that non-violent politics is either too slow or ineffective a method of transforming society. They argue that people only become politically effective when they become active, and when the activity they engage in is violent. We therefore have to be careful that we do not simply equate terrorism with left-wing politics. Its central feature is the use of violence which, at various times throughout history, has been the policy of groups of all political persuasions. Between the First and Second World Wars, for example, terrorism was engaged in by parts of the fascist political movement. The Romanian Iron Guard were involved in the murders of two Prime Ministers. The Nazis in Germany engaged in many acts of terrorism both before and after they took office. Opponents, both within the Party and outside, were beaten and killed.

Many nationalist leaders, like Jomo Kenyatta of Kenya, emerged from violent conflicts with colonial powers to become president.

Nationalist struggles

Immediately after the Second World War terrorism became associated with the nationalist struggle for independence from colonial rule. Nationalists fought the colonial powers for control of their own countries. These political groups followed the example of Mao Tse-tung, who led a long guerrilla war to gain control of China. The guerrillas were based in the rural communities. The towns were the centres of political power, but the guerrillas built up support in the countryside and used this base to overthrow the established authorities in the towns. Acts of terrorism were part of the overall policy.

This strategy was adopted by many nationalist groups. In Kenya in the 1950s, for example, the Mau Mau murdered white settlers and blacks who did not support them. Among the Mau Mau was Kenya's first president after

independence, Jomo Kenyatta, who was imprisoned by the British authorities for his nationalist activities. The Algerian National Liberation Front engaged in acts of terrorism in its fight against French colonial rule and suffered terrorist attacks in return. The nationalist groups built up their support in the countryside, making only occasional attacks on the towns until the time was ripe for a more extensive uprising.

In South America, it was opposition to the economic domination by the USA and Europe which led to the forming of guerrilla groups. These revolutionaries believed that the South American countries were being kept poor in order that the USA and Europe could enjoy even greater affluence. Revolutionary groups emerged, committed to gaining greater financial independence from the Western capitalist economies. The major success in South America was the Cuban revolution of 1959,

Fidel Castro (left) emerged as leader after the Cuban Revolution. The revolution inspired many people seeking social change in the 1960s. (Right) Another of the Cuban leaders, Che Guevara, became a symbol of revolution.

whose leaders, Fidel Castro and Ernesto 'Che' Guevara, became the symbols of revolution for a generation of people in the 1960s.

Attempts to export the Cuban model of revolution to other countries proved unsuccessful. In many of the South American countries, the guerrillas were city dwellers who found it hard to gain support from the rural peasants. They also faced stiff opposition from the military regimes which controlled many of the countries. An uprising in Guatemala was crushed in 1962. Guevara was killed in Bolivia in 1968 after attempting to provoke a guerrilla war, for which he found little support.

By the mid-1960s, there were many rurally

based guerrilla movements attempting to gain either national liberation or social revolution. In some cases, such as in Vietnam, both goals were pursued. When terrorism moved from the countryside to the towns and from the developing world to Europe and the United States, international concern grew.

Carlos Marighella

Urban guerrilla warfare began to evolve in South America, with kidnappings, bank raids and killings. The most well-known of the urban guerrilla groups is the Tuparmaros of Uruguay, but probably more important is the Brazilian Action for National Liberation and, in particular, its leader, Carlos Marighella. Marighella, who was shot dead in 1969, wrote the Mini-Manual for Urban Guerrillas. This was published all round the world and became a key text for many groups of urban guerrillas. It is the basis from which terrorism of the 1980s grew.

In western Europe and the USA, the 1960s saw the development of protest movements, particularly concerned with the American war in Vietnam. Large numbers of people, especially students, sought radical changes in their countries and also in the relationship with the poorer countries of the world. Che Guevara became the symbol of the revolutionary change which many young people were looking for. When all the demonstrations and protests did not result in a radical change, a disillusionment with established forms of political protest set in. It was at this time that Marighella's book was published in Europe, and groups began to form who were committed to promoting radical change by violent means. It is as a result of such links between political movements in the developing world and disillusioned radicals

In the USA opposition to the war in Vietnam was the base for much discontent, even among the veterans of the war.

in the West that international terrorism emerged.

In tracing the evolution of terrorism, it is important to note that many who are taken to be the forerunners or supporters of terrorism would not necessarily have supported the activities of urban guerrillas. For Mao and Guevara the idea of an urban guerrilla would probably have been seen as inconsistent and misguided, because both saw the countryside as the essential base for a successful revolutionary struggle. Once the guerrillas had taken control of large rural areas the towns would fall. In towns this strategy cannot work. It becomes impossible to build up widespread

In Paris, 1968, students rioted due to disillusionment with the failure of social upheavals to create real changes.

support among the population, although, no-go areas do exist in places like Belfast, Northern Ireland. In towns guerrillas have to remain anonymous to avoid detection. It therefore becomes difficult to work alongside the people, as Mao and Guevara imagined. Many who have supported acts of terrorism as part of guerrilla war would oppose urban guerrilla warfare, because acts of terrorism become the only method of warfare.

3 Terrorists or freedom fighters?

The argument that terrorism is always unjustifiable is untenable.

Walter Laquer

I am from a group that decided on self-sacrifice and martyrdom for the sake of the liberation of land and people.

Sana Mahaidali, Shiite suicide bomber

Freedom fighters, rebels, guerrillas, resistance movements, terrorists – these are all terms used to describe the factions in an armed conflict. Ronald Reagan, while President of the USA, called the Contras, fighting the Sandinista government of Nicaragua, freedom fighters. The Soviet Union calls them terrorists. It may often appear that any group which the United States government calls freedom fighters, the Soviet Union will call terrorists and vice versa. Sometimes the superpowers agree. For instance, both have had their citizens kidnapped and killed by Shiite Muslim groups in Lebanon, which they have both condemned as acts of terrorism.

Which term we use to describe a group is very important, because it can colour our perception of that group and its activities. For instance, to call someone a freedom fighter is to suggest that they are promoting the freedom of the people who support that person. We may think this to be a good goal and therefore support the activities of that person. If we call the same person a terrorist, because they employ violence to promote their cause, we may withhold our support.

It is for these reasons that many groups which

Menachim Begin, former Prime Minister of Israel, was previously involved in violence against Britain's occupation of Palestine.

engage in political violence have titles which people will associate with positive values – the Palestine Liberation Organization, the Liberation Tigers of Tamil Eelam, the Irish National Liberation Army. They and their supporters will refer to members of the group as freedom fighters, rebels, liberators, guerrillas. Opponents will call them terrorists in order to show their activities in a different light. We have to try to go beyond the general debate about terrorism in an attempt to establish when and if it is correct to refer to a certain group as terrorists. It has often been said that one person's terrorist is another's freedom fighter. While this is far too simplistic, it does make the point that the way in which we describe groups is not always as clear cut as we may like to believe.

We are all familiar with the way world leaders regularly condemn terrorism. This blanket condemnation is not always helpful to the understanding of terrorism, particularly when many ex-terrorists become leading politicians and vice versa – Menachim Begin in Israel and Robert Mugabe in Zimbabwe, for example. Begin was a leader of the Irgun Zvai Leumi, one of two groups which fought the British control of Palestine in the 1930s and 1940s. These groups engaged in bombings and killings in the same manner as many contemporary terrorist groups. In the 1970s Begin became Prime

Zimbabwe only gained full independence and majority rule in 1980 after a long and bloody guerilla war.

Minister of Israel. Robert Mugabe spent many yeas leading a guerrilla war against the white regime of Ian Smith in Rhodesia before becoming the first black Prime Minister of Zimbabwe after independence had been obtained.

Terror is an aspect of all conflicts, large and small. In a full-scale war between nations, people live in a state of fear, never sure whether a bomb or missile will land on their home or workplace, uncertain of the future. What is specific to terrorism is that it *aims* to create that state of fear and uncertainty.

Defining terrorism

A major problem in the discussion of terrorism is establishing a generally accepted definition of it. This has been one of the main reasons why organizations such as the United Nations have had great difficulty in drawing up effective policies to combat terrorism. Agreement cannot be reached over which groups are terrorists and which are not. Each definition has included groups which many countries do not consider to be terrorists at all. It has often been

Yasser Arafat is leader of the PLO.

cautiously suggested that terrorism is the international use of political violence for social change. This incorporates many groups which many would not necessarily believe to be terrorists, such as the rioters who have been so effective in promoting change in South Korea. But if we accept that it is not an ideal definition, it does help us to understand three principal forms of terrorism – those groups working within a larger political movement; conspiratorial groups working alone; state terrorism.

Those terrorist groups fighting to support and promote the aims of a wider political movement are usually seeking national liberation or greater autonomy from the central state. Examples include the PIRA in Northern Ireland, the ETA in Spain, the African National Congress (ANC) in South Africa, and the Tamil Tigers in Sri Lanka. All of these groups have a military and a political wing with varying levels of support among the communities they seek to represent. Probably the best known is the PLO,

21

led by Yasser Arafat. The PLO is made up of several groups which co-operate in an attempt to obtain an independent Palestinian state. The creation of Israel in 1947 led to the flight of many Palestinians from what had previously been their homeland. After the Six Day War of 1967 in which Israel easily defeated the armies of its Arab neighbours, the Palestinians saw little chance of reclaiming their homeland. To draw attention to their plight, they began to carry out hijackings and other acts of violence outside the Middle East.

As time went on, some of the groups within the PLO, such as Arafat's Al Fatah, began to work in diplomatic as well as military ways in order to promote their aims. Others felt this was a betrayal of the Palestinian cause and supported a military struggle alone. In the 1970s, the most active of these groups was the Popular Front for the Liberation of Palestine led by George Habash. The Abu Nidal group has been move active in recent years. They

Patricia Hearst, American heiress, was initially kidnapped by the SLA but they later involved her in undertaking bank robberies for them.

have murdered PLO representatives as well as committing acts of terrorism against non-Palestinian targets.

The results of using terrorism have been mixed for the PLO. It is now widely recognized as the body representing the interests of the Palestinian people. But, constant Israeli military pressure and wavering support from some of the Arab countries have resulted in the Palestinians being spread around the Middle East and North Africa in refugee camps. The prospect of a Palestinian homeland looks no nearer and the refugee camps produce a constant flow of new recruits prepared to fight for that homeland.

The conspiratorial terrorist groups who work secretly together without any direct links to a wider political movement, largely came into existence in the prosperous capitalist democracies of Western Europe and the USA in the late 1960s and 1970s. Their aims were to support political movements in the developing world, and promote revolutionary change in their own countries. Frustrated by lack of political change, these groups largely consisted of well-educated members of the middle class. Terrorism was used to expose what was felt to be the oppressive nature of capitalism and to support the struggles of the Vietnamese against the USA and the PLO against Israel.

There have been, and still are, many groups which belong to this category: the Japanese Red Army, the Weathermen in the USA, *Action Directe* in France and the Italian Red Brigades. One group which came to prominence in Europe in the early 1970s was the West German Baader-Meinhof group, later to become known as the Red Army Fraction. Andreas Baader was imprisoned for placing fire bombs in a Frankfurt store to protest against the American war in Vietnam. Ulrike Meinhof and several of Baader's friends arranged his escape. Initially, they were able to find support and safe houses among other radicals. As the group began to engage in bank robberies, bombings and the killing of police, support became less widespread. It was not long before the leading members were captured and imprisoned. Baader and Meinhof later committed suicide in prison.

Members of the Red Army Fraction. The R.A.F. was one of the most active of the new groups in the 1970s.

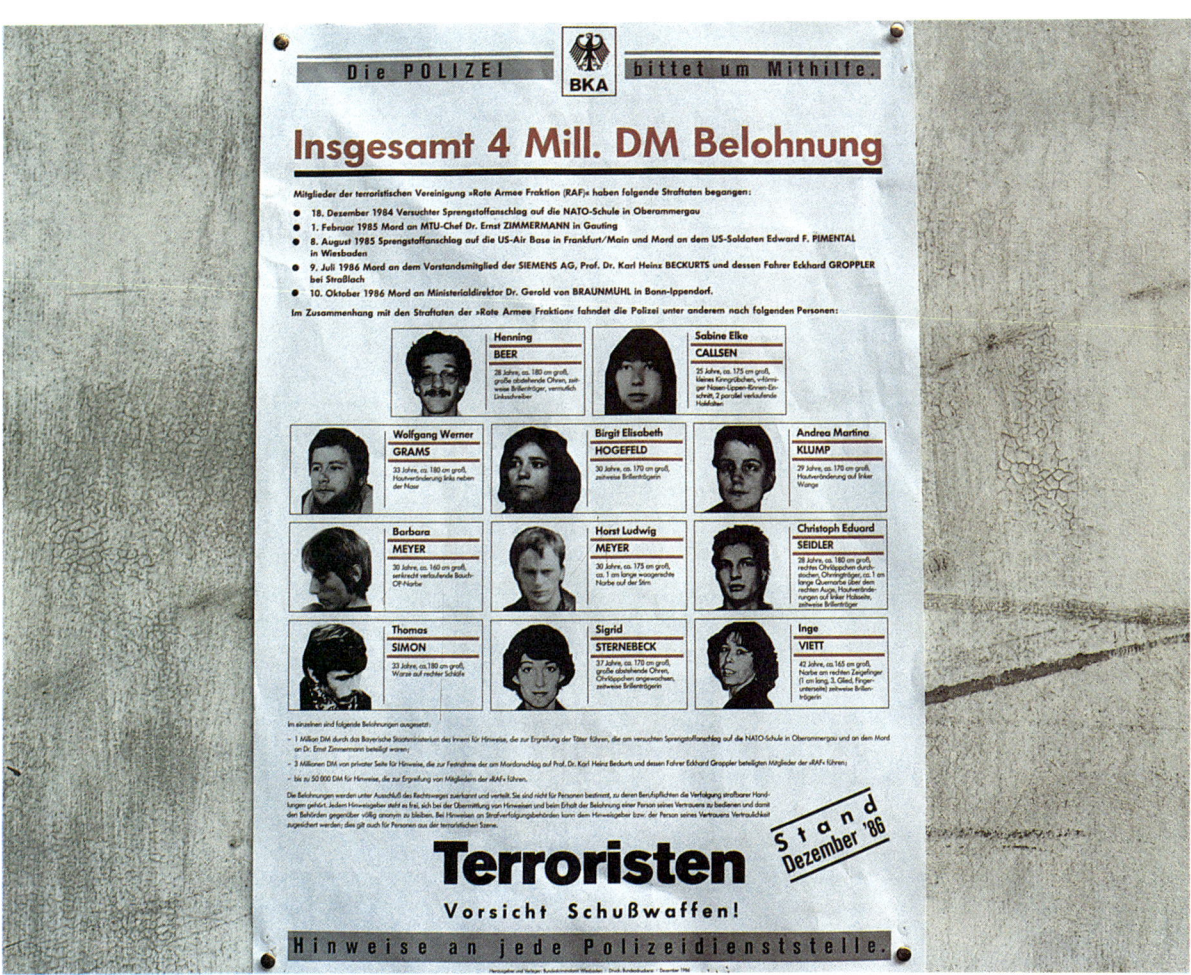

The programme of terrorism they had begun was continued by other members of the group. Most notable was the kidnapping and eventual killing of the industrialist Hans-Martin Schleyer in 1977. Many people consider the acts of terrorism engaged in by groups such as the Red Army Fraction to have been positively harmful to the cause of radical social change. They argue that instead of undermining the power of the state, terrorism has increased popular support for stronger policing and tighter security measures. This has made change harder to achieve.

The third category of terrorism which is gaining greater prominence is state-sponsored terrorism. This usually relates to countries such as Libya, Iran, Syria and North Korea. Most countries provide political and military support for groups who engage in acts of terrorism. The USA provides political and military support to the Contras in Nicaragua. South Africa supports the Renamo (Resistencia Naçional Moçambicana) guerrillas in Mozambique. Mossad, the Israeli secret service, has probably engaged

For many, Colonel Qadhafi of Libya is at the heart of state-sponsored terrorism.

in the assassination of Palestinians living in Europe. The Soviet Union supports many liberation groups around the world, and has been drawn into support for acts of terrorism.

So we have to be careful when governments outwardly stress their opposition to terrorism. They may condemn certain forms of terrorism, but often they are also supporting groups which may be considered terrorists by others. Terrorism has made it possible for governments to wage war against one another by proxy, that is, without direct conflict between the armies of the countries involved. In supporting and sponsoring terrorism, governments seek to promote their own interests at the expense of those of another country.

Terrorism is a very complex phenomenon. These three major forms of terrorism are not mutually exclusive. National liberation movements may work jointly with conspiratorial groups. These operations may well be supported by countries who are interested in promoting the aims of the terrorist groups. For instance, the PFLP and Baader-Meinhof group worked in close co-operation, as well as receiving training and support from the governments of North Korea and Cuba.

(Right) President Reagan of the USA adopted a tough stance against countries he believed to be promoting terrorism.

(Below) In Nicaragua supporters of the Sandinista government have been in conflict with anti-government Contras.

4
Using terror

There are many reasons why political groups attempt to bring about radical social change. People often feel frustrated or angry about their position in the world. They may feel persecuted and oppressed in some way, perhaps as a racial minority, or for religious reasons, or because they feel exploited by colonial rule. For any group engaging in terrorist activities, the reasons are powerful and complex. Let's look at four examples.

It was largely for political reasons that the Italian Red Brigades engage in terrorism. The Red Brigades have been very active throughout the 1970s and 1980s despite the arrest and imprisonment of many of their leaders and activists. Disillusioned by the failure of the strong Italian Communist Party to promote radical change in the interests of working-class people, the Red Brigades engaged in bombings, shootings and kidnappings. Their aim was to provoke a military response to their activities. This would inspire the working people to rise up in support of the Brigades and overthrow the state. The building of a socialist society could then begin.

For the Provincial Irish Republican Army (PIRA) it is nationalist feelings which have lain behind their use of terrorism. The whole of Ireland was originally a British colony and the Irish fought a long battle for self-government. The creation of Northern Ireland left a perma-

In Italy in 1978, captured members of the Red Brigades were put on trial for terrorist offences carried out in 1975.

In Northern Ireland riots against the police and army are a common occurrence. In the London-derry riots of 1969 youths threw petrol bombs.

nent sore among many members of the community who consider themselves Irish, not British.

After the failure of the civil rights movement of the Catholic minority in the late 1960s terrorism attacks began in Northern Ireland, and the British Army was sent in to protect the minority from the Protestant majority. The Army, however, soon became associated with Protestant and London control of the province. The IRA began carrying out their terrorist attacks in support of the minority community. The 'official' IRA soon gave up the use of terrorism, to be replaced by the 'Provos' (PIRA) who have continued a bombing and shooting campaign in Northern Ireland and mainland Britain in support of the reunification of Ireland. Terrorist tactics are also employed by Protestant parmilitary groups such as the Ulster Volunteer Force (UVF) in order to maintain the union with Britain.

In South Africa, it is ethnic factors which lie behind the conflict. The majority of the population is black, but the white minority keeps political power through the system of apartheid, which excludes blacks from participating in the decision-making procedures of the country. The ANC is the principal arm of black resistance (although multi-racial in its composition and outlook). Initially it sought to obtain the participation of the black majority by non-violent means. As a result, their leaders, including Nelson Mandela, were imprisoned and protests crushed at Sharpeville in 1960. Passive resistance had failed. The ANC then formed Umkhonto we Sizwe (Spear of the Nation), a military arm, to carry the fight to the white government. To begin with they bombed property, but as the crisis in South Africa deepened, so bombs and landmines were used against people. This included the 1985 bombing of a Durban shopping centre.

(Above) The township of Soweto in South Africa has seen active black opposition to apartheid.

(Below) The death of protestors at Sharpeville in 1960 led the ANC to move from peaceful to armed opposition.

With the overthrow of the Shah of Iran by the Ayatollah Khomeini, the rise of Islamic fundamentalism has spawned a variety of groups engaging in terrorism. The Shiite Muslim sects which support the Ayatollah seek the creation of states which strictly follow the teaching of the Qu'ran, the main religious text of Islam. Shiite groups oppose all things non-Islamic, in particular the USA and countries of Western Europe, which they consider to be decadent. They also seek to overthrow any pro-Western Arab government. So, to work towards these ends, they have carried out bombings, kidnappings and hijackings, and are particularly active in Lebanon. Most dramatic have been the suicide bombers, often teenagers, who are prepared to drive vehicles loaded with explosives to certain targets before igniting them.

Why terrorism?

Why certain political groups become terrorists, and whether they are justified in doing so are important issues. For example, it may be

Radical Islamic groups such as the Mujaheddin have taken terrorist acts to further extremes in an attempt to further their cause.

argued that the ANC, have a just cause and no alternative to the use of violence, so we may feel that the use of certain acts of terrorism is justified. With the PIRA and Red Brigades, many would argue that becuase they exist within countries which have a liberal democratic system of government through which change can be promoted, terrorism is not justified.

This raises one of the most important issues in the discussion of terrorism, the fact that groups using terror can operate more easily within democratic states than in non-democratic ones. In some Communist bloc countries and highly dictatorial regimes, such as Chile, terrorism has been very limited or non-existent – although the governments themselves have imposed terror on their populations. Problems arise, as democracies rely on certain degrees of freedom of expression and movement, which can be exploited by the terrorist. If you have unrestricted movement and are not constantly under surveillance, it is far easier to organize crimes against the state.

Terrorist groups are electorally weak. If they were strong, they would be able to achieve their aims through the democratic procedures. For instance, the PIRA are not able to obtain a majority vote in Northern Ireland in favour of the reunification of Ireland, so they pursue campaigns of terror to make the North too much trouble for the British to govern. They hope that in the end the British government will want to be rid of the trouble of governing the six countries of the north.

Terrorism and the media

Publicity is an important function of terrorism. Acts of terrorism are by their nature news. The more spectacular the act, the more television and newspaper coverage it obtains. This brings the group's grievances to national and international attention. This would be impossible in countries where the press is strictly controlled or censored. For instance, it was only after 1967, when the PLO began to carry out hijackings that the problems of the Palestinians became a major focus of international concern and interest.

Does the guarantee of media coverage actually encourage terrorism? Are acts of terrorism stage-managed for the media? During the hijacking of the American TWA 727 to Beirut by members of the Islamic Jihad in June 1985, press conferences with the hijackers and the hostages were arranged. This caused widespread concern that the media was allowing itself to be used as a propaganda tool by the Shiite hijackers. It is sometimes argued that the media should reduce its reporting of terrorist incidents, but this raises important questions about the freedom of the media, an essential element of a democracy. But not all publicity is good publicity. News coverage may highlight a cause, but it can also make people more hostile to the terrorist groups rather than encourage support for them.

In June 1985 at Beirut, Lebanon Captain Testrake and 38 passengers and crew, were held hostage for 17 days.

Terrorism can also have the opposite effects of those intended. For instance, in June 1987, there was a huge demonstration in Barcelona, Spain, against the bombing of a supermarket by the ETA. They subsequently apologised for their 'mistake'. Similarly, in South Africa, the upsurge of black violence in the 1980s resulted in the whites digging in their heels against change in their country. In November 1987, a bomb planted by the IRA killed innocent civilians in Enniskillen, Northern Ireland, as they attended a Remembrance Day parade. Revulsion against the bombing has been widespread

Hooded Shiite Muslim hijackers held a news conference to explain their cause, after releasing the 39 hostages on the TWA jet at Beirut.

among Catholics north and south of the border and the Sinn Fein, the political wing of the IRA, has suffered a set-back as a result.

Some terrorist groups have actively sought this kind of backlash, particularly those operating within democracies. They argue that political democracy gives the impression that people are free, when they are really ruled by the oppressive economic demands of

31

The Mothers of the Plaza De Mayo claim that the Argentinian military government is responsible for their children disappearing.

capitalism. The terrorist attacks are an attempt to provoke the state into exposing its true, oppressive nature. Theoretically, once the people see for themselves that they are not free, they will rise up against the state and overthrow it. This has never happened. Democracy has either remained or been replaced by a military dictatorship. Where democracy has continued to function, the people have been revolted by the acts of violence and given their support for tougher measures to combat terrorism. Where democracy has been replaced by military dictatorship, all opposition has been brutally crushed, as happened to the Tuparmaros in Uruguay in 1971, and in the 'dirty war' in Argentina in the 1970s.

In trying to assess whether a group is justified in using terrorism it is necessary to look at the particular causes and circumstances in which it is operating. Some people would argue that terrorism is never justified. However, if all channels for seeking just aims are exhausted and a group has political support for its activities, may acts of violence be justified? Indiscriminate terrorism is another matter. We need, therefore, to be cautious about some of the wild generalizations we hear from political leaders representing all sides of the argument.

5 Combatting terrorism

Terrorism has been seen as a major problem since its emergence in Western Europe and the Middle East in the late 1960s. While acts of terror were confined to conflicts in the colonies and ex-colonies of the major European powers, it did not cause much alarm. The growth of terrorism on a wider scale upset that complacency.

There have been three principal responses to terrorism by governments and government agencies worldwide. The police and the military responses have been the most vigorously pursued. In many cases, the political response has been ruled out altogether. World leaders such as Ronald Reagan and Margaret Thatcher, for example, have stated that they do not believe in negotiating with terrorists and that acts of terrorism should be treated as crimes rather than political crimes. Successive British governments have refused to grant imprisoned PIRA members the political status they demand.

But governments' official policies do not always tell the whole story. A recent scandal,

Britain's Prime Minister Margaret Thatcher, seen here the day after an IRA attempt to kill her, has spoken out strongly against terrorism.

In 1976 the Israelis raided Entebbe airport to rescue hostages. The Israeli pilot received a hero's welcome on his return from the raid.

surrounding the American government's attempt to trade arms with Iran, in exchange for the release of American citizens held by Shiite groups in Lebanon, shows that a government's handling of terrorism maybe more complicated than is at first apparent.

In the early 1970s hijackings and kidnappings were often carried out to obtain the release of people who had already been imprisoned for acts of terrorism, or for ransom money. Members of the Palestinian Black September movement who were involved in the killings of Israeli athletes at the 1972 Munich Olympic Games were imprisoned, but later released in response to another hijacking. Many governments feared that if they did not accept the conditions offered, more acts of terrorism would be committed as a reprisal. Governments believed that the more people held in prison for terrorist offences, the greater the number of terrorist attacks there would be to ensure their release.

New developments

As time went on, firmer measures started to be taken. Countries began to organize special anti-terrorist police and military units. New laws were enacted. Improved intelligence-gathering techniques were introduced. Information about suspected terrorists was more often shared internationally. These new developments were signalled by the Israeli raid on Entebbe airport in June 1976. An aircraft was hijacked by members of the PFLP and the Red Army Fraction and taken to Entebbe in Uganda. Jewish passengers were then threatened with death. In response, the Israelis mounted a military raid which secured the release of the hostages and the death of the hijackers.

A similar assault on a hijacked plane took place in October 1977. Members of the PFLP hijacked a Lufthansa plane to Mogadishu in Somalia, demanding the release of leaders of the Baader-Meinhof group and 18 million dollars. A West German commando unit stormed the plane, releasing the hostages, killing three of the hijackers and wounding a fourth. Two

34

members of the British Special Air Services took part in this operation. The SAS were to show their own ability in combatting terrorism when the Iranian Embassy in London was occupied by an Iraqi-backed group in 1980. The hostages were released after the Embassy was stormed by the SAS, and the kidnappers were killed.

Not all such operations have been successful. In November 1985, an Egypt Air 737 was hijacked by members of the Abu Nidal Palestinian group. On landing at Luqa airport in Malta, the hijackers began to murder their hostages one by one. The plane was stormed by Egypt's anti-terrorist Thunderbolt force. Unfortunately the plane caught fire during the assault and 59 people were killed.

(Right) Security at major airports like Heathrow, England has been increased in an attempt to clamp down on terrorist activities.

In May 1980 the British SAS stormed the Iranian Embassy in London. The Embassy was under siege by six Iranian terrorists holding twenty-six hostages.

International co-operation

In taking firmer action against terrorism, many countries have sought to increase international co-operation. This has not always been straightforward, even among countries which are normally considered allies. For instance, it is only recently that it has become possible to extradite PIRA suspects from the USA to Britain. Before the agreement, PIRA suspects had been able to claim that their struggle in Northern Ireland was political and obtain political asylum in the USA. Political asylum provides immunity

The Palestinian hijackers of the ship Achille Lauro were caught and imprisoned in Italy.

from extradition. Also, many groups engaging in terrorism base themselves in countries, such as Libya, with whom there may be no treaty governing the extradition of suspected terrorists, or little basis for general co-operation in responding to terrorism.

Even within NATO, the Western military alliance, differences of opinion about how to respond to terrorism undermine international co-operation. This was particularly noticeable in the response to the pirating of the cruise liner *Achille Lauro* by members of the Palestinian Force 17 group in October 1985. The terrorists surrendered to the Eygptian authorities

and were provided with a plane to fly them to Tunisia. The plane was intercepted by American jets and forced to land in Italy. The Americans wanted to take the pirates to the USA, but were prevented by the Italian authorities who arrested them themselves. This caused a major diplomatic row between the American, Italian and Eygptian governments. The American government felt that its action had been justified, while the Italians and Eygptians were severely embarrassed by the incident.

The closer co-operation and greater consistency in policy between countries in responding to terrorism has resulted in a more effective police and military response than in the early 1970s. However, large problems still exist due to the particular situation of different countries and the varying outlooks of their governments.

Political solutions

While there has been a good deal of activity by the police and military in responding to terrorism, political responses to the grievances which lead to terrorism have been less forthcoming. Many people argue that if a political solution to a conflict is provided, the reasons for using terrorism disappear. For instance, in India, Sikh groups in the state of Punjab want to form a separate state not controlled by the government in New Delhi. The Indian government is resisting such moves, so the Sikhs have started to carry out acts of terrorism to promote their aims. It could be argued that if the Indian government was to grant the Sikhs political and economic autonomy, there would be no need for the Sikhs to become terrorists.

Such arguments are much too simple. Most conflicts are far more complex than the above picture suggests. For instance, what would happen to the non-Sikh population of the Punjab? What happens to those Sikhs who prefer to remain under the control of the Indian government? Would a self-governing Punjab be able to support itself economically? If one region is allowed independence, how many others would wish to follow? Questions and problems abound. The same would be true of the Palestine/Israel conflict. The creation of Israel deprived the Palestinians of their homeland. To give them back that homeland would deprive the Jewish community of their country. Political solutions are not always as easy to obtain as some people suggest.

In India, Sikhs demanding a separate Punjabi state have resorted to violence to try to further their aims.

For instance, since the return of democracy to Spain, the Basque region has been granted a greater amount of autonomy. At the same time ETA has increased its demands to such an extent that the Spanish government feels incapable of responding further. Secret negotiations have taken place between the two sides, but it is going to be difficult to reach an agreement that will hold. Equally, it will be difficult to crush those who will not renounce violence, without alienating the Basque population. This shows that a political solution to a conflict depends upon both sides wanting a solution. If a group makes demands which are incapable of being met or is itself split over policy, a political solution becomes almost impossible.

The problems of responding to terrorism are far greater in countries with democratic forms of government. In authoritarian and dictatorial regimes martial law can be imposed and all forms of opposition suppressed. In democracies care must be taken to ensure that the

The Spanish Basque separatist movement ETA have been offered some political concessions but still continue their campaign for a separate state.

The British police at the IRA siege of Balcombe Street, London adopted a tactic of forming a relationship with the gunmen in order to persuade them to give themselves up.

measures taken to combat terrorism do not undermine the freedoms which are essential for democracy to function. If it is necessary to relinquish a lot of freedoms to combat terrorism, the result could be a more repressive non-democratic regime, the type many groups seek to promote as the first stage of revolution. Body searches and the checking of baggage at airports may be acceptable. But arrests without trial, trails without juries and interrogation techniques which border on torture raise fundamental questions about the future of democratic countries.

Terrorist acts tend to be spectacular, but their impact on the everyday lives of people around the world is very limited. For the groups using terrorism it is important to exaggerate its effects to show that they are being effective in promoting their aims. Governments may exaggerate the problem of terrorism in order to justify more respressive measures which can

Tamil Terrorists came looking for the brother . . . . Since he was away, his sister Miss. Amarasingham Yogarani (24 years) was dragged out of the house, tied to a coconut tree and shot through the ear

WHY ARE GUARDIANS OF HUMAN RIGHTS SO SILENT?

then be used against all forms of opposition. This has been particularly true in some South American countries where terrorism was used by military regimes to suppress all opposition. It is also true to a lesser extent in democratic countries where stricter controls have been accepted as the price for combatting terrorism.

It is essential that political solutions are worked forwards if we want to avoid dictatorial governments. Political solutions may be harder to obtain than military victories, but without

Publicising terrorist acts can help governments in combatting terrorism. The Sri Lankan government released this picture to try to discredit Tamil separatists.

political responses terrorism is unlikely to go away. So far military action has been seen to be the effective response to individual incidents, but groups engaging in terrorism are as active now as they were in the early 1970s.

6
Terrorism, present and future

You can run, but you can't hide.
Ronald Reagan in response to the Achille
Lauro piracy

We are the soldiers of God and we crave
death . . . Violence will remain our only
path.
Statement issued by Islamic Jihad

In 1976 over 3,000 people attended the burial
of German terrorist Ulrike Meinhof, proving that
terrorists are not always unpopular.

Terrorism is still with us and is likely to remain.
Due to increased airport security, hijackings
may not occur as regularly as they did fifteen
years ago, but they still take place. Measures
to combat bombings may have become more
sophisticated, but so have the bombs. Some
terrroist groups have slipped into the shadows,
such as the Weathermen. Others, such as the
Japanese Red Army, have given up using terrorist tactics. However, many groups continue
to use terrorist methods and new groups have
been formed.

Older Nationalist groups, such as ETA, the
PLO and PIRA continue their struggle for self-
rule. They have been joined in recent years
by groups within the ex-colonies of Western
European states seeking greater freedom from
central government in the regions. The two
most notable examples are the Sikhs in India
and the Tamils in Sri Lanka. There has also
been an upsurge of activity by Armenian
groups in Turkey seeking to force the Turkish
government to acknowledge guilt for the mass
slaughter of Armenians during the First World
War.

Many of the groups operating within Europe

The American bombing of Libya in 1986 received criticism and opposition from many countries. Will terrorism act as a spark for wider conflict?
Good relations between the USA and Soviet Union may assist international co-operation in responding to terrorism.

have now lost their original leadership, either through imprisonment or death, but they still remain active. The Red Army Fraction and the Red Brigades continue their campaigns and have been joined by new groups, such as *Action Directe* in France and the Communist Fighting Cells in Belgium. These groups now tend to focus on NATO targets and American personnel, and have shown signs of sophisticated co-ordination across Europe.

South America has seen the emergence of groups such as the *Sendero Luminoso* (Shining Path) in Peru and M-19 in Columbia. M-19 has been accused of narco-terrorism, protecting the drug traffickers who grow, process and export cocaine from Colombia, in exchange for money and arms.

The most important development in terrorism in the 1980s has been the growth of Islamic fundamentalism. Shiite groups have replaced the Palestinians as the major force in promoting terrorism. Supported by countries such as Iran, Syria and Libya, these groups have engaged in acts of terrorism against Western interests, Arab states which are pro-Western and even the Palestinians themselves. There has been the growth of numerous groups, each with its own allegiances and aims, mostly based in the Lebanon. As with the PLO, these groups are generally referred to under the umbrella term, Islamic Jihad (Islamic Holy War). Different groups have different interests which they pursue, but they are all committed to Islamic fundamentalism and are prepared to die for the cause, in the belief that they will go straight to heaven.

As the contacts between groups engaging in terrorism and states supporting their aims have increased, the fear has grown that war between states is the inevitable outcome. In certain circumstances, this has already occurred. In the 1970s and early 1980s, the Lebanon

New groups of terrorists constantly emerge. Jean-Marc Rouillan (left) and Nathalie Menison (right), leaders of Action Directe, were France's two most wanted guerrillas.

was used as a base by Palestinian groups for attacks on northern Israel. In 1982, Israel invaded the Lebanon with the purpose of removing all Palestinians. A bloody conflict followed which resulted in the vast majority of PLO supporters being forced to flee overseas. However, the Israeli invasion caused a great deal of resentment amongst the Shiite population of the Lebanon. Thus, while the Israelis were relatively successful in removing the Palestinians, they now face terrorist attacks from Shiite groups.

It was the fear of a possible war which led to criticism of the American air raid on Libya on 15 April 1986. The Americans blamed the Libyans for organizing an attack in a discotheque in Berlin in which American servicemen were killed. In retaliation they bombed targets in Libya – partly with the use of F1-11s based in Britain. This caused widespread concern among America's allies, as there were questions raised about the proof of Libyan involvement and about the legality of the reprisal. The raid caused extensive damage

and the death of civilians, which created a good deal of support for Colonel Qadhafi among Arab countries.

There is much concern expressed about American support for the Contras in Nicaragua. It is felt by many people that a conflict between Nicaragua and the USA would result in a similar war to that experienced by the Americans in Vietnam.

The spread of nuclear weapons and manuals explaining how to make them, may mean that it will not be long before a terrorist group threatens to explode a nuclear device. There is much argument about the likelihood of this happening but most believe it would be too complex for a group to produce, and the unpredictable effects of a nuclear explosion would make it an unattractive terrorist weapon. The same is also true of chemical weapons, the effects of which are devastating and equally unpredictable.

Terrorism is a problem which will not go away. In order to understand it, we have to look at each situation in detail and, as a result, attempt to make appropriate responses. Where terrorism is unjustified, it is necessary to isolate the group from people who may support it and take effective measures to capture those engaging in such acts. This may mean satisfying some of the political demands of the group. If

The supreme court at Bogota, Colombia was taken over by M-19, a group believed to be funded by the smuggling of drugs.

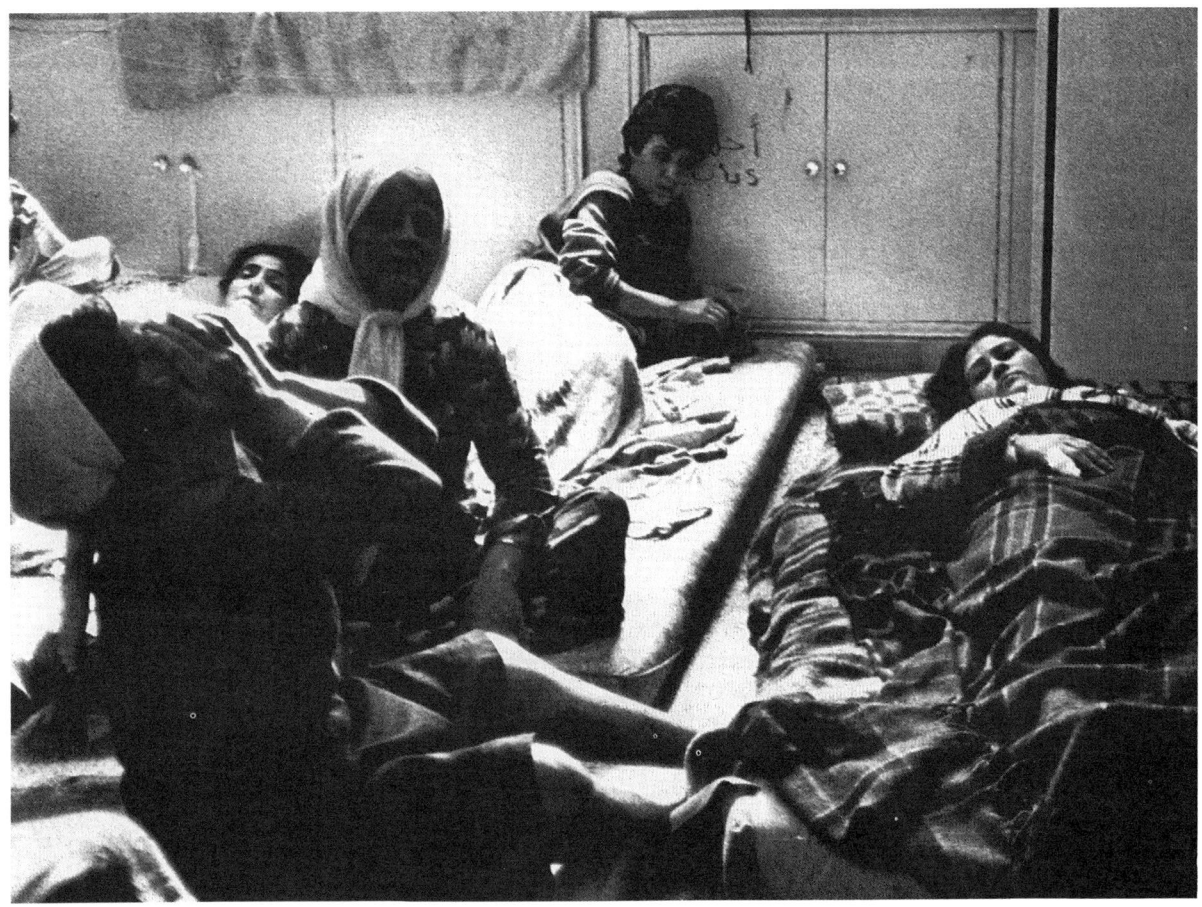

groups are isolated from potential supporters, it is far harder for them to operate without being noticed and informed upon. On the other hand, if the use of terrorism is seen as justified, we will face the hard decision of whether or not to support the group, or even become a member of it.

A greater willingness from nations and governments to respond to the grievances which result in terrorism and more international co-operation in intelligence gathering can help overcome terrorism. However, the ideological and nationalist tensions in international relations make co-operation almost impossible to achieve. Groups engaging in terrorism seek radical social change in many forms. There are always others who oppose and will continue to oppose such changes. So, terrorism is likely to remain with us for the foreseeable future. We should not look at it as a problem in isolation; we must look carefully at the different circum-

A Palestinian refugee camp in the Lebanon. In the 1980s Palestinians have been the victims of Shiite Muslims. Terrorism can affect anyone.

stances in which terrorism is used. This is a complicated procedure which should avoid any generalizations which can result in dangerous simplifications. If we are too simple in our appreciation of a specific form of terrorism, we may respond totally inappropriately, creating an even worse situation than the one with which we started.

The principal danger of terrorism in the 1980s and 1990's is that it can be the spark for a major war between nations, as in 1914, even if it is unlikely to be the cause of such a world conflict. Until such time as greater thought is given to terrorism in its many forms, that possibility will remain with us. There are no easy solutions to terrorism; in fact, there may be no solutions at all.

Glossary

Action Directe   An Anti-NATO group using terrorism in France.

African National Congress   Major movement of black resistance to white domination in South Africa.

Anarchists   People who believe in society without a state.

Assassination   The murder of a prominent political leader or public figure.

Baader-Meinhof Group   A West German group using terrorism in the early 1970s. After its leaders were imprisoned, it became known as the Red Army Fraction.

Capitalism   The economic system based on private enterprise in a free market, and individual profit.

Colonialism   The conquest and settlement of one country by another.

Communism   An economic system based on common ownership, forming a classless society.

Democracy   A system of government accountable to the people.

Dictatorship   A form of government where absolute power lies with one leader or a small group.

Euzkadi ta Azkatuzuna   Basque separatist organization.

Guerrilla   A member of an irregular army, usually operating in the countryside.

Hijacking   Seizing something, usually a means of transport, by threat or violence.

Imperialism   The domination of one country by another for economic, political or strategic reasons.

Irgun Zvai Leumi   A Jewish terrorist group that fought the British control of Palestine in the 1930s and 1940s.

Islamic Jihad   The umbrella organization for Islamic fundamentalist groups.

Marxism   Karl Marx's theory of historical change based on class struggle and the means of economic production.

Nationalism   The desire for self-government of a country by its people.

Palestine Liberation Organization   The umbrella organization founded in 1964, which represents the Palestinians in their fight against Israel.

Provisional Irish Republican Army   A nationalist group fighting British control of Northern Ireland.

Red Brigade   An Italian terrorist group.

Renamo   Another name for Resistencia Naçional Mozambicana.

Separatist   A person who promotes the establishment of independent regions, free from central government control.

Shiites   One main branch of Islam now centred on the regime of the Ayatollah Khomeini in Iran.

Umkhonto We Sizwe   The military arm of the African National Congress.

Books to Read

Jonathan Bearman, *Qadhafi's Libya* (Zed Books, 1986)

Julian Becker, *Hitler's Children* (Michael Joseph, 1977)

R. Clutterbuck, *Living With Terrorism* (Faber, 1978)

Christopher Dobson and Ronald Payne, *The Carlos Network* (Coronet, 1978)

Christopher Dobson and Ronald Payne, *The Terrorists, Their Weapons, Leaders and Tactics* (Fact on File Inc., 1982)

Christopher Dobson and Ronald Payne, *War Without End* (Harrap, 1986)

David Hayes, *Terrorists and Freedom Fighters* (Wayland, 1985)

Walter Laquer, *Terrorism* (Abacus, 1978)

Walter Laquer, *The Age of Terrorism* (Weidenfeld and Nicolson, 1987)

Walter Laquer, *The Terrorism Reader* (New American Library, 1978)

Philip Steele, *The Tactics of Terror* (Macdonald, 1986)

Claire Sterling, *The Terror Network* (Weidenfeld and Nicolson, 1981)

Paul Wilkinson, *Terrorism and the Liberal State* (Macmillan, 1977)

Index

Numbers in **bold** refer to illustrations

Picture Ackowledgements

Associated Press 30; Camera Press 10 (bottom), 15, 17, 19, 21, 24, 25 (bottom), 28 (top), 35 (top), 35 (bottom), 39, 42 (top), 42 (bottom); Mansell 13, 14; Popperfoto 7 (top), 12, 26, 27, 34, 36, 41, 43, 44, 45; Rex cover, 6, 38; Frank Spooner frontispiece, 29; The Research House 20; Topham 7 (bottom), 10 (top), 11, 16 (left), 16 (right), 18, 22, 25 (top), 28 (bottom), 31, 32, 33, 37, 40; VISNEWS 23; Artwork by Malcolm Walker.